If found please return to...

Made in the USA
Las Vegas, NV
16 December 2022

62968417R00057